MARSHA SINETAR

Why Can't Grownups Believe in Angels?

Triumph Books Liguori, Missouri

Published by Triumph™ Books

Liguori, Missouri

An Imprint of Liguori Publications

Library of Congress Cataloging-in-Publication Data

Sinetar, Marsha

Why can't grownups believe in angels? / Marsha Sinetar.

p. cm.

ISBN 0-89243-551-8 : $14.95

1. Angels—Juvenile literature. 2. Sinetar, Marsha. I. Title

BT966.2.S54   1993

235'.3—dc20   93-12906

                                               CIP

                                               AC

ISBN: 0-89243-551-8

Printed in the United States of America.

First Edition

10 9 8 7 6 5 4 3 2 1

In honor of my grandmother,
Memere, who must still be
surrounded by enduring good.
With gratitude for her tender,
nonintrusive love
and encouragement.

It is our fundamental, primary job to help all children feel at home, and safe, in the world. Fairy tales, myths and folk tales teach children in symbolic, fantasy fashion that evil and virtue coexist, must be dealt with, and are essential parts of life. It seems quite another matter (and a dangerous one at that) to deprive children of a belief in the existence of enduring good.

Most parents easily enthuse about Santa Claus, the Easter Bunny, Charlie Brown's Halloween Pumpkin, and even give "Tooth Fairy gifts" to sustain joyful make-believe as long as possible. Surely the time has come for good guardian angels to contribute to positive child-rearing.

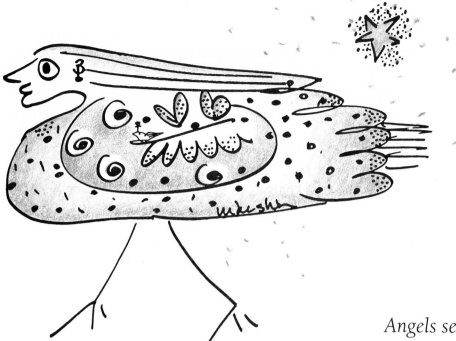

Angels seem the perfect child-
hood imagery, and the guaranteed positive,
spiritual archetypes, to accompany children through
the ups and downs of their young life. Before children can unquestionably
trust in the joyful, good guardianship of angels, their parents have to
believe in them—even be willing to talk about them in some credible way.

Why not remind ourselves of the teachings in both the Old and the
New Testament which describe the supernatural benefits and reality of
angels? (You might find the Afterword of help on this.) By doing so we can
bring uplifting, wholesome ideas to the minds of young children.

This book is based on a true story. As a little girl, the author had visions of angels. She trusted in their faithful protection and friendliness, despite hearing her sophisticated parents discount such notions. Here we meet a child who wonders why almost all grownups possess her parents' conventional logic.

nce upon a time, years and years ago—
when I was just a tiny child—a sparkling-bright
angel befriended me.

She came around mostly at bedtime.

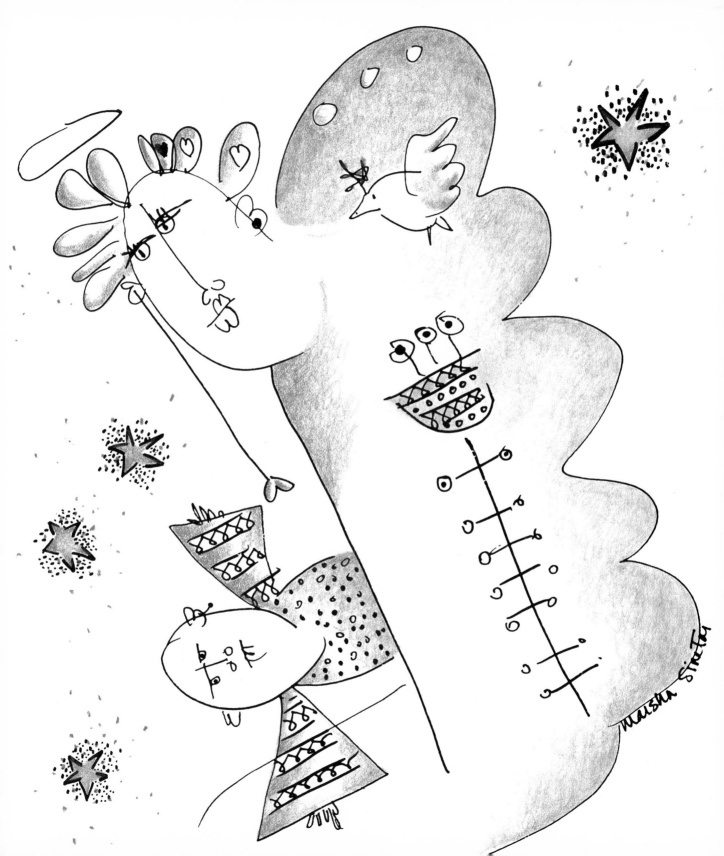

In radiant white-light and deep, stunning silence, she perched nimbly at the foot of my bed. She lounged in a neighborly way (with perfectly lovely posture, I might add), sitting amiably as if on the air itself, right at the tip of my carved oak footboard.

Somehow (but don't ask me *how*) she sang her purposes directly into my soul, leaving this silvery-voiced message in my being:

I'm one of God's ministering angels—your life's special guardian and devoted friend.

Well, you can imagine my delight—how marvelously glad I was to make her acquaintance. I felt honored to bask in her sunshine gaze and wise, all-knowing countenance. Her yellow-gauze curls misted fragrant, gold glows. She had long, slender fingers that seemed (to me at least) rays of pure morning light, and as I say, a jujube perfume smoked all 'round her presence.

Every night for the longest time, she'd beam into my world. Even when I didn't *see* her, I sensed her watching peaceably over me. She reclined at my feet, hazed in lollipop-scents and pale shine, until I fell asleep. (One of her most agreeable qualities was that she asked nothing of me. You know how rare this is.)

Of course, at first I was simply too overjoyed and excited to sleep. (Who wouldn't be?)

Eventually, though, I'd float off into the most delectable slumber—full of safe, candied feelings and warm, cozy dreams. I treasured this. I needed this.

Alas, if anyone at all entered my bedroom— *especially* a grownup—she'd vanish in the blink of an eye, with lightning-flash speed. I felt her absence keenly.

Maybe she left because she suspected that no one would believe me if I said I'd *seen* an angelic presence. Perhaps she was meant to appear only before my eyes. Or, it could have simply been her proper time to leave. I've learned since that most endings happen quite naturally. Probably much like you, I don't like good-byes and certainly didn't appreciate hers.

Whatever her reasons for coming and going, I tell you dears of this (and other ministering angels) in case you should ever need help.

Believe this: God's good angels are *meant* for us, sent to us to bear us up in their bright, graceful hands.

Their main job is to watch over us lest we dash ourselves against life's harsh, jagged spots. Doubt provokes them. Unbelief keeps them at bay.

Darlings, all this is nearly forgotten, almost secret information, so tuck it away in your heart. It's important. The particulars could come in handy some day.

Dear ones, my personal experience was precisely as follows:

None of the grownups around me would hear of angels. (You know how logical adults try to be, how they always insist that we be sensible too!)

Being no fool, after a time I kept all my special sightings to myself. At first, I tried discussion.

"Oh no, darling," my dear father gruffed softly, wrapping me snugly in starch-shirted, sweet-scented arms,

"You're only imagining things. Angels do *not* exist. Whatever gives you such odd, old-fashioned notions? Now just close your eyes and go to sleep. That's a sweet darling… "

marsha

Obediently, I'd close my eyes, exactly as Father instructed. But the instant I did, I felt a sharp dread—some shadowy twist of my mind. Then, bingo! Here came all sizes and shapes of glowing good angels, mobilized tunefully into place. They deployed themselves in sparkling array— purring melodically at every turn. I was in awe: every false, eerie thought gave way to their strategically delicate shine. (How I treasured these moments. How I needed them.)

You see, angels were my youth's special blessings. They gave me great stores of hope and grand, lucid visions of pure, wholesome love.

Like sun arc soldiers bedazzling me to safety, their incandescent energies clarified and protected my life's path.

But no one else received their twinkling gifts. Then when I was alone I'd wonder, "Oh, why can't grownups believe in angels? What keeps people so far, far away from their good?"

I could have convinced my mother, although I didn't try.

"It's probably just a dream, *Mon Petite Chou*," she'd whisper while tucking me in at night, quaintly sprinkling in a light phrase of French now and then (since that was her native tongue).

Then she'd fold cool, fresh-pressed sheets about my shoulders and stroke my brow warmly in that gentle way most mothers have. (How I loved *these* moments. How I needed them).

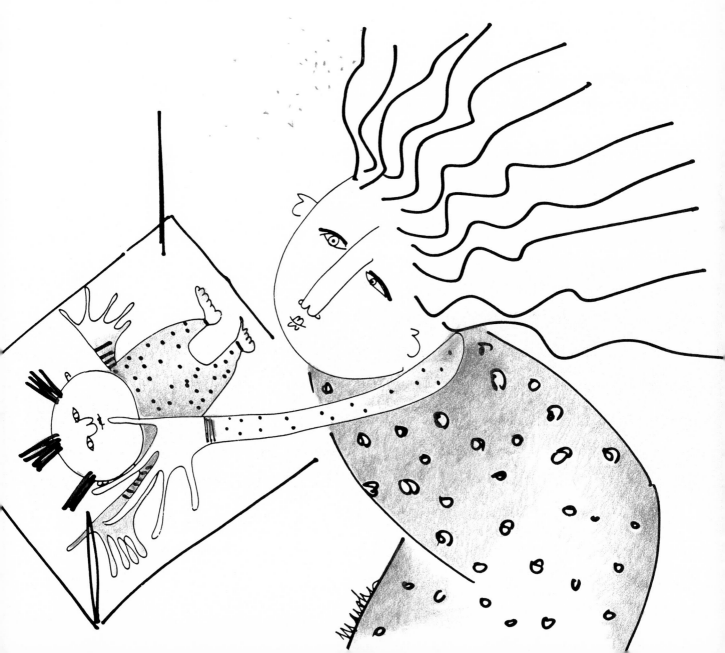

"But that's all right, *Mon Amour.* It won't hurt you to dream about angels. I did that a bit myself when I was little. Just don't take your dreams too seriously."

On that settled note, with great dignity, she'd glide out of the room, satisfied that she'd put me—and all talk of angels— to bed once and for all.

So I'd close my
eyes obediently, exactly
as Mother had instructed.
All alone again, and drifting off to
sleep, I'd think, "How will I *see* angels if I don't take them
seriously? What keeps grownups so far from their good?
Oh, why won't they believe in angels?"

The years passed, as years are meant to do. And I eventually grew up.

I stopped seeing that one particular angel (you know, my bedtime angel), and certainly I stopped *talking* to anyone about angels or even wondering why people didn't believe in them.

But—and this really seems the important point to tell you—I didn't stop *believing* in good angels. Not for a single solitary moment.

Nor did angels ever stop ministering for me, even after I grew up.

Here is exactly what happened.

Remember it well:

Once, when I was fully grown and utterly defeated (I can't remember exactly *why* anymore—you know how gloomy adults can get), an $\mathcal{ENORMOUS}$ angel flared over the threshold of my door in a radiant, thundering chariot.

It was early, early morning, and I'd just had the thought that there was little reason to get out of bed, when woosh! The giant glowing angel burst in on me. On his head sat a chandelier crown—all ablaze in gold flames and pure essence of myrrh.

His church-organ voice commanded me, "Arise and eat." Musically, he introduced himself: *"I'm Fred."*

Then Fred prodded me on—although I must say I followed his instructions quickly, as I'd done with my parents' directives. He told me to have a bite.

I had a tuna-fish sandwich, a cup of chicken-rice soup, and a large helping of chocolate pudding served in my favorite blue-and-white porcelain bowl. Then I fell back into a deep, restful slumber.

Twice more that huge, luminous angel returned. The second time, he repeated his orders: "Arise, eat. You lack strength for the things you want to do. Proper food and rest will revive you. Harken this rule for your future."

Again, I did as I was told.

I ate two sweet, fresh pears and three hot-buttered scones and drank four steamy cups of milky rich cocoa. In due time, I saw that the big angel was right: I did regain vigor, and hope as well, and was fine in no time—able to continue with my life.

The sheer, sparkling memory of Fred's fiery good humor stayed with me, restoring my faith in good things and kind people.

Yet a *third* time an angel came
to me. I can't say if this one was a
boy or a girl or a man or woman.
I can tell you it was incandescent—a
veritable moonbeam wearing a
headdress of birthday candles and a gown
of sheer bell-like stars. Its torchlight eyes pierced through my
mind, but—as it fairly *reeked* of caramel fudgies—I
wasn't a bit afraid.

Its heavenly dazzle snapped me to attention (and, of
course, I was swimming in sweet fudgey fragrance).

This wondrous, chocolate-scented light form was flanked by a chorus of bright little cherubs in various shapes and forms. Their rock-n-roll harmonies cheered me up. But within myself I pondered, "Why are they all here? What do they all want?"

Eagerly, I awaited instructions. Instantly it seemed, on the heels of my question I knew my answer:

You see, my dears, I'd been wrong—had gone quite totally astray (selfish and unloving) for who knows how long. Alas, I hadn't had the courage to change.

To make matters worse, I'd been all alone in my trouble—with no one to talk to and grieving to the core.

The night before, when I'd said my prayers, I had vowed to turn myself around, as my conscience dictated I must.

This new band of angels now shone into my life, dancing and twirling and rejoicing together in a triumphant celebration.

Their angelic, glad sounds were like hundreds of twinkling wind chimes. This further softened my heart and moved me to love my goodness.

At that instant I knew that all would be right with my world and with me from then on. Such was the charm of their twinkling tribute.

To this day, even when I'm not actually *thinking* of angels, small, ordinary events will bring them to mind, like

—rainbows and moonbeams and shy,
   friendly birds

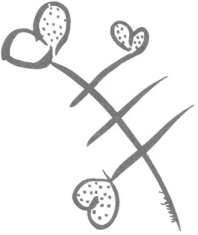

—and Christmas and Easter and
   birthday parties

—and talks with dear friends and hugs and
   square dancing, and of course, caramel fudgies
   and the sound of wind chimes!

These instantly bless me with angelic remembrances and shift my thoughts toward possibilities of good times.

Then I'm infused with new courage or inexplicable joy—completely certain once more that God's unfathomable agents know us, guard us in our comings and goings, and bear us up in their sweet, shepherding way.

Dear ones, I now tell you one thing for certain: since before the mountains were created, and from everlasting to everlasting, angels watch over children (both big and little).

They help grownups too, particularly those who are lost or afraid—

—and all the more so if we believe in them.

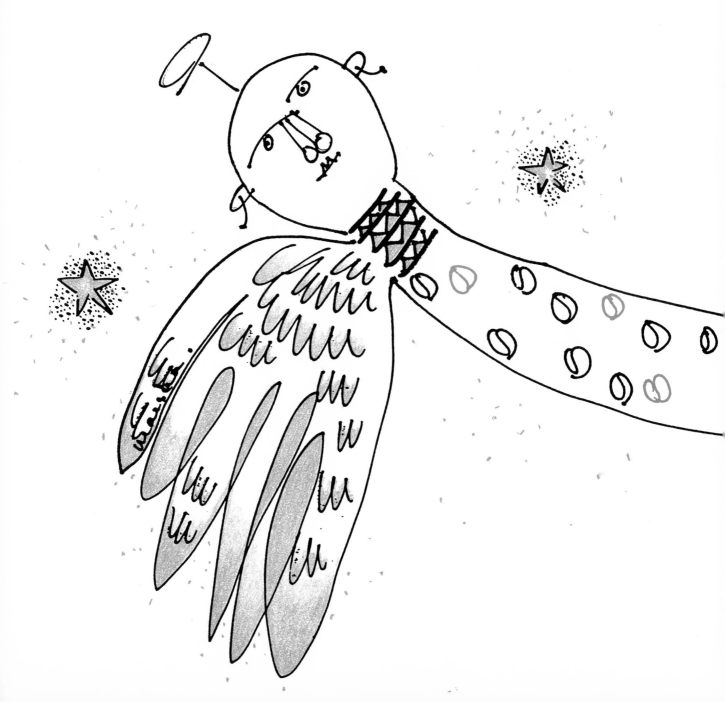

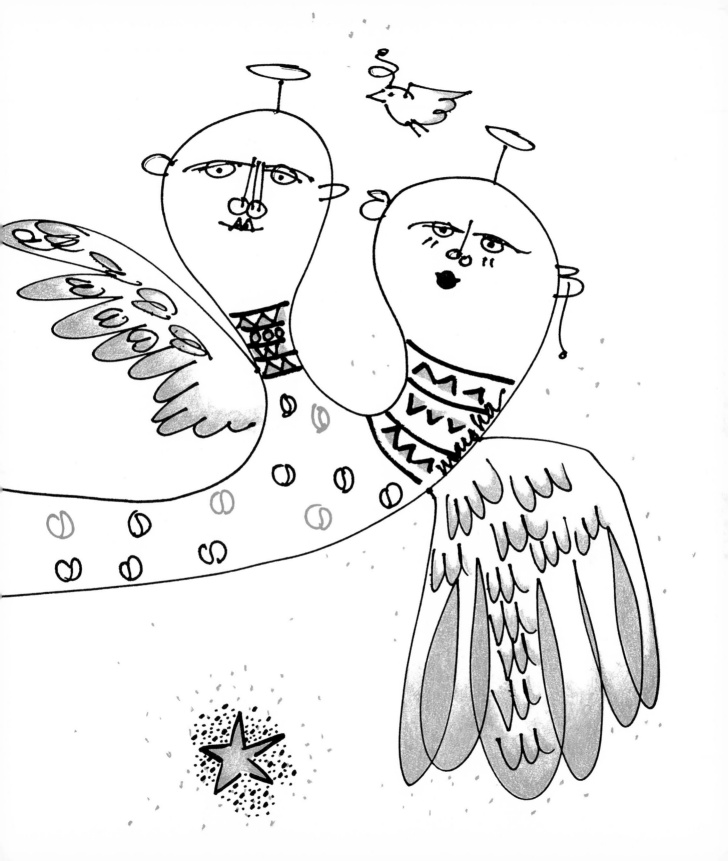

That's why from time to time, I still wonder: what
keeps some of us so far from our good and why, oh why,
can't *everybody* (and especially grownups) believe in God's
heavenly angels?

THEY ONLY SHOW UP FOR OUR GOOD!

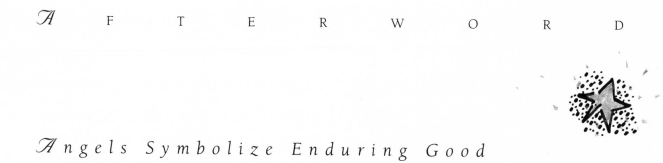

A n g e l s   S y m b o l i z e   E n d u r i n g   G o o d

A child's unconscious is shaped by images and sounds. Today nearly all of these pictures violently assault a child's awareness, leaving unique and lasting imprints. The best parents methodically build a child's faith in the reliable existence of enduring good. We hear that modern-day youngsters live a lonely life under a shroud of fear. Talk of all-out war, the destruction of the earth's delicate, exquisite ecosystems, and the victimization of children are common to children's lives. We think nothing about sharing such gloomy information with tiny children, perhaps unaware that they form their self-view (and their view of the world) by what we adults say.

Play, fiction, and language lessons either build lasting mental well-being or can undermine stability at an early age. Given the world's historic, natural emphasis on whatever is unpleasant, parents have their jobs cut out for them. Could it hurt to balance the dark, foreboding side of the storytelling scales with positive, hopeful news? This is how we tilt perception toward life's promise and properly support children's growth.

A child's unconscious will not properly structure high self-esteem, optimism, or the possibility of practical success if fears and anxieties are unresolved. Fairy tales further this resolution by describing the destruction of the evildoer or by showing children how heroes and heroines use courage, truth, and other virtues to overcome bleak, unhappy circumstances. As agents of God's love, and as unseen protectors of little children, angels can be important emotional helpmates in a child's unconscious.

The first time the storyteller meets an angel in adulthood, her experi-ence is far different than when she was a child. Now she is worn out and worried about something (we don't learn what it is). Parents may wish to draw out their children's feelings about their own worries or fears.

Since 1 Kings 19: 5-6 was used as a framework for this first adult meet-ing with angels, it is a good idea for parents to familiarize themselves with this section of Kings prior to discussing the story with their child. In this passage, we find Elijah has achieved a public victory, but he is threatened by Jezebel for daring to confront her. When Elijah can bear no more of this struggle, he prays for death, asking God to take his life. Instead, God sends one of his angels to Elijah as he sleeps under a juniper tree. The angel advises Elijah to rest, eat, and gain renewed strength so that he can continue to live productively.

In this same spirit, parents can help children understand the simple wisdom that this angel presents: there are times when we all have been (or will be) discouraged, so worn out that we *think* we cannot continue. By resting, taking a respite from our worry, or by just eating properly and generally getting away from things, we too will be regenerated. This amounts to biblical stress-management advice, and certainly we can profit from it.

The storyteller also meets an angel in adulthood when she admits she has made unproductive choices. After she realizes this, and changes her ways, angels appear in great numbers, all of them rejoicing about her choice to live a proper and well-ordered life. Here the angels' happy welcome underscores Luke 15: 1-10, "… there is joy in the presence of the angels of God over one sinner who repents." We change for the better when we consciously turn away from what we know is hurtful or wrong.

Whatever a child's circumstances, gentle conversations about angels can remind a youngster that God is loving and that, mysteriously, the world can be a happy, safe place. The philosopher Eli Siegel once wrote, "… liking the world is the greatest instinct of our unconscious." People of all ages (and especially children) long to believe in their good futures. Considering that we most easily nourish this instinct in a hospitable atmosphere of ideas, one still wonders why everyone—particularly grownups—can't believe in angels.

Marsha Sinetar's fertile imagination and whimsical, fine-line drawings reflect her well-known interest in the creative process—a fascination that finds expression through a remarkable spectrum of books, illustrations, lecturing, and corporate activity.

From her remote forest home along the Northwest coast, Marsha Sinetar—a bestselling, internationally acclaimed author, educator, and corporate psychologist—strongly influences contemporary thought about the issues of optimal personal growth. Sinetar's dedication to wholesome personal development at every level animates the best in people of all ages and defines the bright array of all her work.

Her pen-and-ink illustrations capture the sharp-edged, feeling state of childhood, and testify to the artist's extensive early professional background as one of those pioneering, nurturing educators we instinctively want for our young. Her spare, primitive images reveal a boundless, loving universe where few distinctions or troubles exist, where possibilities are unlimited, where people communicate freely (and with all manner of creation), and where we each can express our own lively feelings—the heart of our own creativity.

Marsha Sinetar's artwork

is available from *Henley's Gallery*

at The Sea Ranch, CA (707-785-2951)